STEVE PARISH · **WILDLIFE** · AUSTRALIA FROM THE HEART

Contents

A Western Grey Kangaroo rim-lit by the late afternoon sun.

WILDLIFE FROM THE HEART

Ever since, as a child, I first saw photographs of animals in National Geographic magazine, I have been besotted with wildlife. The first animal that had an impact on me was an African Lion at the zoo in Adelaide. Then I discovered marine fish, a group of creatures that I have watched, stalked and photographed now for forty years.

Ever since those early experiences in nature's wild places, I have followed my dream to explore Australia in all its fascinating variety, photograph it, and share my discoveries with others. This book and its associated CD-ROM is part of that sharing experience, and I do hope that they convey to you the joy that my journey's have brought me.

Steve Parish

Western Grey Kangaroos, alert to danger.

MAMMALS

Australia's mammals are not as plentiful and perhaps not as dramatic as those found in other continents, but they more than make up for all this with their spellbinding behaviour. Most species are nocturnal and, therefore, their study presents a considerable challenge to photographers, researchers, rangers and general observers alike. However, with a little basic understanding, the challenge is well worth accepting, and Koalas, kangaroos, possums, gliders, wombats, Dingos, whales and dolphins can all be observed with relative ease.

A Koala sets out in search of tasty gum leaves.

Few can resist the attraction of a young Koala.

KOALAS *eat eucalypt leaves, which have low energy content. And so Koalas sleep for up to 20 hours out of every 24. Their bodies are admirably suited to life in the trees, and the dense, grey-brown, woolly fur is waterproof. Each fore paw has two thumbs, and all digits have strong, sharp claws. Koalas live alone, except when nursing young or mating. A male Koala claims a territory that may include areas of the home range of several females. The male calls loudly to attract females that are ready to mate.*

Learning about life on mother's back.

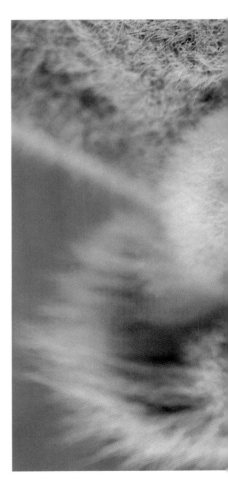

After a night of grazing, this young Common Wombat dozes in the warm, early-morning sun, beside the entrance to its daytime lair.

Northern Hairy-nosed Wombat, above right; Common Wombat, below.

W O M B A T S *are active at night and during sunny winter days. They eat native grasses, shrubs and roots. Each wombat lives alone, but the burrows it digs may connect with those of other wombats. A big burrow may be up to 20 metres long, with several chambers and entrances.*

As I approached, the rustling grass soon brought this pair of Eastern Grey Kangaroos to an upright listening posture.

An Eastern Grey Kangaroo carries her large joey.

KANGAROOS carry their joeys in the pouch for 11 months and then suckle them for a further 11 months. A reserve embryo may then develop when the pouch is vacant.

Grey kangaroos live in mobs and prefer to feed in the early morning and late afternoon, which, of course, makes them great subjects for photography.

WALLABIES and kangaroos belong, with tree-kangaroos, to the group known as "macropods". The populations of smaller species, the nailtail wallabies and the hare-wallabies, have dropped enormously due to habitat loss, competition from rabbits, sheep and goats, and introduced predators like the European Fox and the feral cat. The grass-eating kangaroos, wallaroos and larger wallabies have benefited from tree-clearing to improve pastures and the provision of water troughs for stock.

This young Red-necked Wallaby and a Common Wombat adopted each other in a fauna park in Tasmania.

A large male Red Kangaroo in one of its many leisure postures.

The Green Ringtail Possum of north Queensland curls into a ball to sleep on a branch.

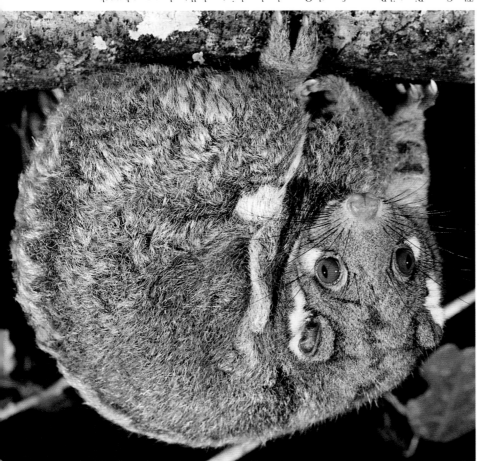

TROPICAL rainforests, particularly in Australia, support some of the world's most unusual and threatened mammal species. On these pages are just two of the rare animal species found in this green wonderland. Finding and photographing these specimens was a big challenge, but it was well and truly worth it!

Bars of yellow, white and black on each fur fibre give the greenish tinge to the Green Ringtail's coat. The Lumholtz's Tree-kangaroo has developed shortish, broad back feet and powerful fore limbs that help it to climb trees.

A young adult male Lumholtz's Tree-kangaroo. These animals mainly eat leaves, but will also eat fruit, which they hold in both front paws.

Dingos bonding.

DINGOS are primitive dogs that evolved from the Indian Wolf. It is still unknown how they came to Australia, but it was probably with South-East Asian fishermen between 3500 and 4000 years ago. Dingos quickly spread over mainland Australia, and Aborigines just as quickly began to use them as hunting dogs and companion animals – a Dingo makes a good blanket on a cold night in the desert! It seems that the Dingo, which did not ever reach Tasmania, hastened the extinction of Tasmanian Devils and the Thylacine on the mainland.

The biggest threat to the Dingo is the breakdown of its gene-pool caused by interbreeding with domestic dogs. Already the purebred subspecies is disappearing in the south-east highlands. The knowledge that this race is under threat adds sadness to the satisfaction of catching a good photograph of a Dingo.

Dingos inhabit all of Australia's wild ecosystems, from the coast to the desert.

Numbats, which feed during the daytime, have highly developed senses of smell, sight and hearing.

This Numbat has paused to soak up the warming rays of the early morning sun.

NUMBATS *feed on termites, but cannot tear open termite mounds: they scratch open termite runways or pull apart soft, rotting wood, licking up the insects with their long tongues. A female Numbat has four young in January, carries them around for 5 months, then feeds them in a nest for another 5 months. The Numbat is one of the few marsupials that feeds during the daylight hours. They are extremely alert, never straying far from the den, which may be in a hollow log, tree or burrow.*

TASMANIAN DEVILS

are Australia's largest marsupial carnivore. They were found on the mainland until around 430 years ago, but are now found only in Tasmania, and are most common in the north-east of the island. They spend the day in a den. From dusk to dawn they scavenge dead animals, and hunt insects and small mammals. In April, 2–4 young are born and are then carried in the mother's rear-opening pouch. After 16 weeks they are left in the den while she finds food. At 40 weeks of age they can survive on their own.

Rival Tasmanian Devils will often display, jaws agape, to threaten each other.

The Platypus is, without doubt, Australia's most unusual wild creature.

MONOTREMES

are extraordinary! It is not surprising that English scientists thought they were being conned when the first specimen of a Platypus was sent back to them. And the Short-beaked Echidna is almost as strange as the Platypus. These two species, together with the Long-beaked Echidna, which lives in New Guinea, make up the whole of the Order Monotremata, and are the only egg-laying mammals in the world.

The Short-beaked Echidna is a monotreme and, like the Platypus, lays eggs.

Common Ringtail Possums have successfully adapted to life in the suburbs.

POSSUMS *of many varieties ornament life in Australia, although city dwellers who share their neighbourhood with possums may not quite agree with me — possums can make an unbelievable din running back and forth across tin roofs! Different species occur in rainforest, bush and arid lands, these tough, agile creatures being well adapted to life in the treetops. Nonetheless, the tiny species such as the pygmy-possums and Leadbeater's Possum need us to protect their habitats.*

The Striped Possum inhabits the tropical rainforests of north Queensland, living mainly on insects.

Western Pygmy-possums feeding on nectar.

A Sugar Glider feeding on a Grevillea blossom.

Sugar Gliders at home in a hollow log.

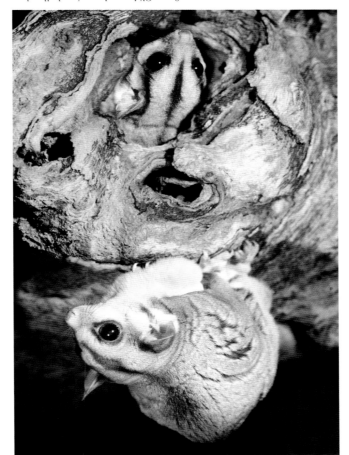

SUGAR GLIDERS *live in tree hollows, in colonies of up to 7 adults and their young. A group recognises its members by scent. At night, the gliders feed on tree sap, nectar, pollen and insects. In cold weather, the group huddles together for warmth and may become torpid.*

A female carries two young in her pouch for 2–3 months. They leave the nest aged 4–5 months. At 7–10 months, young Sugar Gliders leave their group to find a new range. Many do not survive this perilous journey.

Bottlenose Dolphins are highly intelligent and endearing animals.

Sub-adult male Humpback Whales frolicking during their migration south to the Antarctic.

WHALES AND DOLPHINS, with porpoises, are known as cetaceans, and all of them probably evolved from four-legged, land-dwelling mammals that were covered in fur.

The Bottlenose Dolphin ranges widely through the world's seas and is often just as curious about human behaviour as we are about it. Humpback Whales winter in polar feeding grounds and summer in warm-water breeding grounds, migrating thousands of kilometres between the two. Males sing complex songs that carry far under water. My most memorable diving experiences have been with whales and dolphins.

New Zealand Fur-seal pups are often curious about divers and their cameras.

SEALS AND SEA-LIONS, *many of which breed on Australia's southern shores, on New Zealand's coast and around the Antarctic, are incomparable. Certainly no other animals are able to swim and play with such ease. Juveniles are particularly playful and will often stay with a diver for hours on end, peering curiously into the face mask, or tugging on swim fins.*

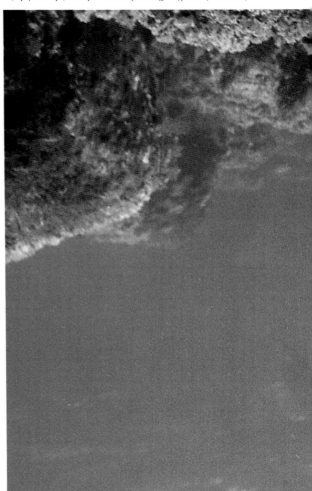

A young Australian Fur-seal comes ashore (above right).

BIRDS

Australia's birds are among the most extraordinary in the world, and some eight hundred species have been recorded. They inhabit all ecosystems from the open ocean to the dryest corner of the desert. They vary in size from the miniature wrens to the enormous Emu and Southern Cassowary. They parade in all the colours of the rainbow — Australia's parrots are world famous for the brilliance of their plumage. Successfully capturing the colours and characteristics of these feathered wonders has been one of my greatest challenges as a photographer.

An Emu struts its stuff on the endless plains of the Outback.

A Jabiru fishing and an egret in flight: part of the magic of a tropical billabong.

A honeyeater bathes in a rain shower at dawn.

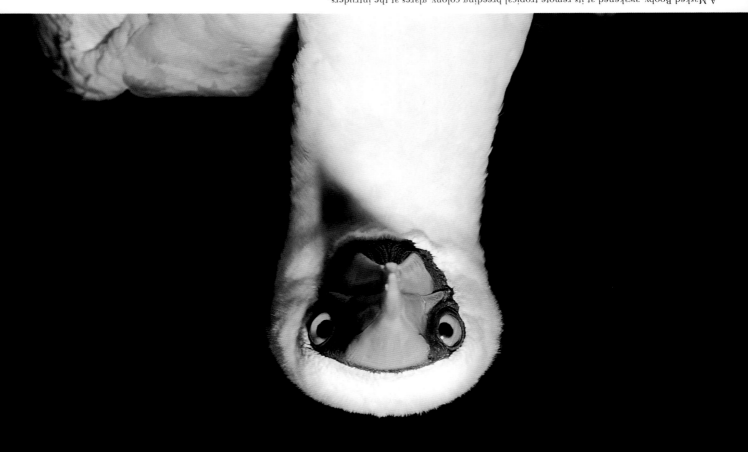

A Masked Booby, awakened at its remote tropical breeding colony, glares at the intruders.

A Black-necked Stork, known as a Jabiru by most Australians, preens its wing coverts and secondary flight feathers.

The Sulphur-crested Cockatoo is famous throughout Australia for its raucous cry.

40

The Crimson Rosella is one of the most colourful parrots.

Rainbow Lorikeets sometimes form huge flocks and are common in coastal Queensland.

The Eastern Yellow Robin camouflages its nest with strips of bark.

The male Regent Bowerbird's plumage is distinctive.

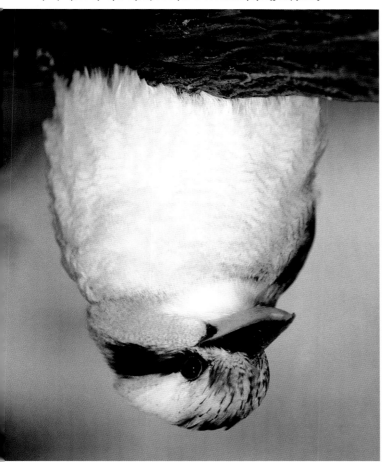

Laughing Kookaburras are as at home in the suburbs as in the bush.

The Rainbow Bee-eater is extremely agile and nimble in flight.

REPTILES AND FROGS

I suppose that romance and reptiles are not words that go together for most people. For myself, I find the match perfect! Few things are more sensuous to touch than a python's lithe skin, are more gentle than the soft pads of a gecko's feet as it climbs up your arm, or more hypnotic than the gaze of a deadly snake – and the smile of a crocodile is guaranteed to hold your attention. "Nuts!" you say, but I am not alone. Thousands of Australians are consumed by their interest in frogs and reptiles, and they have more than 700 species to choose from!

The patterns on Carpet Snakes and Diamond Pythons (different races of the same species) are exquisitely textured.

The Thorny Devil is a small dragon lizard from Australia's arid areas. (Aptly enough, its scientific name is *Moloch horridus*.)

The Southern Forest Dragon lives on the fringes of rainforest.

The Frilled Lizard is Australia's reptilian emblem.

C R O C O D I L E S *are, without doubt, the most feared and respected Australian reptiles. Freshwater Crocodiles do not deserve this reputation, but "Salties" do. Growing to a length of 7 metres, they have been responsible for the deaths of many careless tourists and fishermen in the north. They are skilful hunters and well-practised at stalking their prey – their camouflage is so good that unskilled observers will easily miss them. I well remember an Aboriginal Australian whose crocodile-spotting astounded me. What most alarmed me that he could see a Salty when I saw none!*

The Freshwater Crocodile (above right) grows to three metres long.

A Green Tree-frog displays its endearing "grin".

GREEN TREE-FROGS are far the most popular of the 200 or so Australian species of frog, probably because of their wonderful green skin, and, I guess, their big webbed feet and almost clown-like "grin".

Many of my happiest moments in the wild have been when hunting these creatures with my camera. They are easiest to find during the wet season and, like all frogs, at night. Then you simply detect a croak, aim a soft spotlight at the sound and home in on the eye-shine. The habitats of many species are endangered.

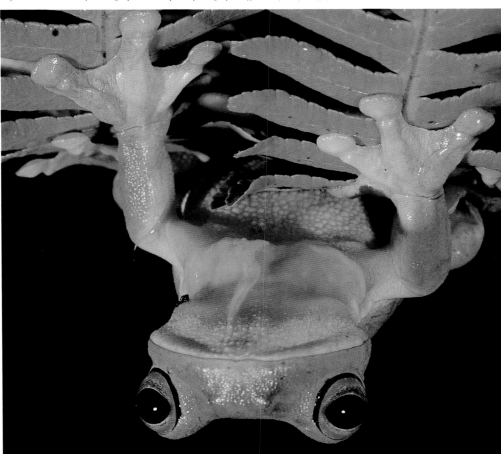

The Red-eyed Tree-frog is usually only found on the ground after spring or summer rain.

A beetle makes its home on its dinner.

INSECTS

Ninety-five per cent of Australia's terrestrial wild creatures belong to the huge subphylum of insects. I agree that we could well, perhaps, do without some, like midges and mosquitoes. However, without insects there would be no other plant or animal life on earth. As a photographer I am most attracted by chances to fit insects into the overall environment, and so I like to photograph them unobtrusively, composing my pictures so that the animal is seen "at home", whether that be on a lily in Kakadu or on a palm frond in the Daintree.

The Cairns Birdwing Butterfly, a native of Queensland's tropical rainforests.

A dragonfly alights on a blade of grass.

Two Painted Sweetlip visit a Cleaner Wrasse's "cleaning station".

MARINE LIFE

Australian marine life has fascinated me for forty years — Australia is blessed with an enormous variety of fish, which is enhanced by the country's diverse habitats, from tropical reef waters in the north to cool temperate oceans in the south and the frigid waters of Antarctica. But the greatest variation is found among the coral reefs of the World Heritage listed Great Barrier Reef Marine Park.

A Pink Anemonefish goggles at me from an anemone's stinging tentacles.

Robust Feather Star.

The tentacle tips of a Giant Sea Anemone.

REEFS, *whether of coral or rock, are where marine invertebrates are most plentiful and diverse. Their behaviour is less understood than that of any other animal on the planet. But it is their incredible forms, textures, colours and shapes that intrigue me as a photographer. Many have developed unique relationships with vertebrate animals.* **The anemone and the anemonefish are perhaps the best known** *examples of this.*

Sunshine Coral with the tentacles extended.

Slipper Corals with their tentacles withdrawn.

An Eastern Quoll with her young. These animals are killed by feral foxes, cats and dogs.

WHAT ABOUT US?

We all dream of exploring strange places
and discovering creatures no one has
ever seen before. I am lucky because I
have been able to live this dream since
my teenage years. However, there is pain
as well as joy in this — negligent
environmental practices have brought
species that I have photographed to the
brink of extinction.

Fauna Parks and captive breeding
programs help to preserve endangered
species, but the animals need to be safe
in the wild. We must all act as
representatives for these mysterious
creatures that have no voice, and ask:
What can we do? What about us?

The numbers of the Bridled Nailtail Wallaby fell to just a few hundred, but are now climbing slowly under a management program.

ALSO IN THE SAME SERIES:

Australia • Wild Places • Brisbane • Melbourne • Sydney

WHY NOT VISIT OUR WEBSITE FOR FURTHER DETAILS?

www.steveparish.com.au

THE STEVE PARISH WILDLIFE

Australia from the Heart

INTERACTIVE CD-ROM

If you have enjoyed Steve's book of Australia's magnificent wildlife, and would like more, we suggest that you look at his stunning Australian Wildlife CD-ROM.

Over 150 wildlife pictures are featured via:

- an interactive STORYBOOK that will take you further into the wonderful world of Australian animals
- a breathtaking SLIDE SHOW set to music
- PHOTOGRAPHIC TIPS to help you take glorious wildlife pictures of your own

- animal CLIP ART to decorate your e-mails and stationery, create your own greeting cards, or illustrate school projects
- DESKTOP PICTURES that will turn your work station into an Australian wildlife panorama
- a SCREEN SAVER picture show
- ELECTRONIC GREETING CARDS
- Steve's own story in MEET STEVE PARISH.

The CD-ROM is both Mac and IBM compatible, and comes with a free download of Quicktime Player 5.

From an early age, Steve Parish has been driven by his undying passion for Australia to photograph every aspect of it, from its wild animals and plants to its many wild places. Then he began to turn his camera on Australians and their ways of life. This body of work forms one of Australia's most diverse photographic libraries. Over the years, these images of Australia have been used in thousands of publications, from cards, calendars and stationery to books – pictorial, reference, guide and children's. Steve has combined his considerable talents as a photographer, writer, poet and public speaker with his acute sense of needs in the marketplace to create a publishing company that today is recognised world wide.

Steve's primary goal is to turn the world on to nature, and, in pursuit of this lifelong objective, he has published a world-class range of children's books and learning aids. He sees our children as the decision makers of tomorrow and the guardians of our heritage.

Steve Parish ™
PUBLISHING

Published by Steve Parish Publishing Pty Ltd

PO Box 1058, Archerfield, Queensland 4108 Australia

www.steveparish.com.au

© copyright Steve Parish Publishing Pty Ltd

ISBN 1 74021 082 4

Photography & text: Steve Parish

Photos: p. 1, Sulphur-crested Cockatoo; pp. 2–3, Australian Pelicans, ducks.

Cover design: Audra Colless

Printed in Hong Kong by South China Printing Co. Ltd

Film by Vakta, Pty Ltd, Australia

Designed and produced in Australia at the Steve Parish Publishing Studios